TRADITIONAL COUNTRY LIFE

STEWS
SOUPS
CHOWDERS

To Sharon –
Enjoy!

Sherlah

TRADITIONAL COUNTRY LIFE RECIPE SERIES

STEWS
❧ SOUPS ❧
CHOWDERS

by Sheilah Kaufman

Cover Illustration: Lisa Adams
Interior Illustrations: Jane Lawrence
Interior Typesetting: Lisa Mars

The Brick Tower Press ®
1230 Park Avenue, New York, NY 10128
Copyright © 1998
by Sheilah Kaufman

Kaufman, Sheilah
The Traditional Country Life Recipe Series:
Includes Index
ISBN 1-883283-15-9 softcover

Library of Congress Catalog Card
Number: 97-74019
First Edition, April 1998

This book is dedicated to the following people because they ate soup—lots of soup: Eileen and Barry Barry, Carol and Michael, Helene and Barry, Sherrie and Victor. And to the ladies in the Group: Carmen, Scotty, Mars, Naomi, Jill, Lily, Amy, Annie, Judith, and Bernie.

TABLE OF CONTENTS

Thomas Jefferson's kitchen at Monticello just a few miles from Charlottesville, Virginia:
As a precaution against fire, Thomas Jefferson situated his Monticello kitchen some distance from the main house. Servants carried meals through an underground passageway.

SOUPS, STEWS, CHOWDERS

Soup's on!

That familiar cry in American homes means "the meal is ready." America is a great melting pot, and this is certainly evident in our cuisine.

In the New World, soups were a mainstay of the diet. Pilgrims existed primarily on soups that had been prepared in large pots that were suspended from overhead beams on the Mayflower. In colonial kitchens, the predominant utensil was a large kettle. George Washington (or his cook) invented Philadelphia Pepper Pot Soup while at Valley Forge as a hot and hearty meal was needed for the troops and while supplies were low after a hard winter. The cook used what was available; tripe, bones, and peppercorns, and named the soup after his hometown!

Since the Pilgrims, the pumpkin has also been part of our American heritage and tradition. Archeologists have found evidence that the pumpkin has been part of the diet (with other members of the squash family) for thousands of years. Pumpkins were a staple in the diet of Native Americans in the north to southern areas as far as the Andes. As tribes migrated, they planted squash, corn, and bean seeds. When grown, they baked or boiled them to make cakes and soups, and ground them to make meal. In Massachusetts, the Pilgrims might never have survived until that first Thanksgiving without the generosity of the friendly Indians who gave them seeds to plant and taught them the different ways to cook pumpkin. The Spanish conquistadors were most likely the first Europeans to see and enjoy them, and contributed to spreading them worldwide throughout Europe to Asia and Africa, during the 16th century.

When President John F. Kennedy addressed a dinner of Nobel Laureates in 1962, he was quoted as saying: "I think this is the most extraordinary collection of talent, human knowledge, that has ever been gathered together at the White House...with the possible exception of when Thomas Jefferson dined alone." Jefferson was our nation's first notable gastronome. Even before his trips to France he imported French wines and other French foods for his table, and was the first to introduce vanilla and macaroni to the United States. He grew the first figs, dates, almonds, and pistachio nuts in the United States, and even introduced French style ice cream. Where ever he was, he was supervising the cooking. He cured one of the best Virginia hams, and took such pride in this that he would not even share the recipe with his daughter when she married! While still a member of the Virginia House of Burgesses, he laid out the grounds and kitchen garden with what was then the largest collection of vegetables, fruits, herbs, and nuts to be found in the colonies. He was famous for his peas. In Amsterdam while trying to negotiate a loan for America, he tasted waffles for the first time, refused to leave the conference table until he was given the recipe, and demanded the address of the best waffle iron maker! One of Jefferson's favorite soups was Pigeon Soup... "A plentitude of these wild birds in the local forest around Monticello," and boiled beef was one of his favorite dishes. (Please turn to page 18 for Jefferson's Pigeon Soup recipe.)

Some General History

Soup's history is hard to trace, but ancient man first made soup when he discovered the idea of filling an empty animal skin bag with meat, bones, and liquid, along with some hot stones to cook the mixture. As time went on, clay containers were used, the ingredients became more varied and were simmered directly over the heat, thus becoming the first pot au feu, or pot on the fire.

For most of world history, hearty soups were the mainstay of family and communal meals. In Sweden, historically, it was the custom to give food and a place to sleep to anyone that came to your door. Usually leftovers from the meal would be dumped into a kettle as a starter for the next night's meal. This is also done in France and China, where drippings from roasts and gravies are saved and used. In making soups, no food scraps should go to waste! One of the earliest references to soup is in the Biblical story of Jacob and Esau, where Esau sells his birthright to Jacob for a "pottage of lentils." Cooks throughout the centuries have utilized whatever was available (from the land and sea), and prepared their foods according to local customs and taste.

Soupe au pain, bread soup from a Middle Age recipe, is prepared by "making a cullis sugar and white wine, ornamented with the yolks of eggs and perfumed with a few drops of rose water. Then toaste lightly a few slices of bread, cut rather thick, and toss them into the broth. When they are well saturated, dip them in a bath of hot oil. Then plunge them again into the broth, sprinkle them with sugar and saffron and serve at once." (Taillevant) In the 15th century, *soupes* were simply sliced bread dipped in broth or wine. Joan D'Arc ate bread soaked in wine both before and after a battle as a stimulant. When housed with a bourgeois family after defeating the English at Patay in 1429, the lady of the house wanted to know what to feed Joan and asked some French officers. The reply was "bread and wine."

In *The Soup Book* by Louis P. DeGoup, published in 1949, DeGoup writes "Soup is cuisine's kindest course, it breathes reassurance; it steams consolation; after a weary day it promotes sociability...there is nothing like a bowl of hot soup, it wisps of aromatic steam making the nostrils quiver with anticipation." In 1765 the first restaurant (an eating establishment) opened in Paris, France, and exclusively served soups. The name restaurant comes from the Latin motto above the entrance which translated to "Come to me all of you whose stomachs cry out and I will restore (*restaurabo*) you."

Broth, Bouillon, Stock, and Consommé

Soups are the most versatile and variable item that can be served, and are synonymous with good eating and satisfying nourishment. Soups may be hot, cold, thick or thin, jellied, puréed, creamed, clear or full of chunky pieces of meat and vegetables. A marvelous soup is more than just something good to eat. In many parts of the world, in many cultures, a hot bowl of soup is a meal; in others, a remedy for a sick person. Soups are nutritious and appetizing foods that can be used in a variety of ways: as appetizers, snacks, a main course, or an entire meal. They are great for a late snack on a cold winter's night. There are hot soups, cold soups, light or heavy soups, thick or thin soups. Cold soups are a bright note in a menu for hot summer days or nights, when you don't feel like cooking, and are not even sure if you want to eat!

The different names that soups are known by date only from the mid 19th century, and many people are still confused by the terms broth, bouillon, stock, and consommé (in fact as far as preparation is concerned, they mean all the same thing–cooks use the terms interchangeably). A broth is a clear soup, its flavor essentially from a combination of meats, vegetables, and herbs that are simmered in water and then strained when the cooking is finished. It can be used as is, or as the base of other soups, sauces, aspics, and is even used to braise and cook vegetables. Bouillon is just the French word, now anglicized, for stock or broth. Broth's predominant flavor may come from beef, chicken, vegetables, or fish, but usually implies beef alone or in combination with chicken.

Stocks are the foundations of cooking, and are made the same way as broth, but are usually used to cook something else in or as a base for a sauce. But, as someone once noted, "stock never goes to the table." A consommé is a perfectly prepared beef broth, and should be richly flavored and completely clear. Cream soups are simply purées with cream added, but if the main ingredient is shellfish, the soup may be called a bisque. Bisque is a very frugal way to prepare expensive crustaceans. In lobster bisque, for example, even the shell is used.

Webster defines soup as a word of Germanic origin, (from *sop*, meaning the bread over which a pottage, broth or other liquid was poured) meaning a liquid

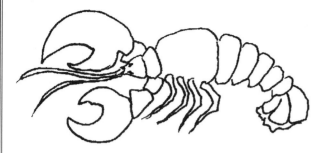

food especially with a meat, fish, or vegetable stock as a base and often containing pieces of solid food. The French word *soupe* is used to describe not a liquid preparation, but various ingredients put into a bouillon or broth, whether made with fish or meat. Today in France, the word *soupe* (as distinct from the more frequently used *potage*) is used to describe a peasant-style soup, where the principle examples are cabbage soup, or various thick vegetable soups, usually garnished with bread.

Bouillabaisse is a famous soup from Marseilles, France, composed of many kinds of fish seasoned with olive oil, garlic, saffron, and tomatoes. Italy, Spain, and other Mediterranean countries have similar versions of this famous soup. Chowder stems from the French "la chaudière," meaning cauldron or big copper pot. Today it means a nourishing soup made from fresh fish, shellfish (or both), vegetables, and seasonings. The most famous American chowder is New England clam chowder. The difference between New England clam chowder and Manhattan clam chowder is (quoting the *American Heritage Cookbook*): "The most famous of American chowders is Clam Chowder, with its 2 essential ingredients: Clams and salt pork or bacon." Manhattan clam chowder calls for water rather than milk and tomatoes. Down Easters were so incensed over the tomato question that the Maine legislature once tried to pass a bill to outlaw forever the mixing of clams and tomatoes! Chowders made from clams and oysters, and of course, corn chowder, are indigenous to our country.

Stone Soup

A children's story, originating in France hundreds of years ago, called *Pebble Soup* or *Stone Soup* tells the story of an old man who walks down the road into a French village. As the villagers are afraid that he will ask for food (vegetables, meat, barley, etc.) they hide everything. The old man is hungry and asks for something to eat and is told there is nothing; it is just a poor village. Then the old man offers to make pebble or stone soup for the village. A large pot is called for, filled with water, and placed over a big fire. Smooth pebbles or stones are called for and are dropped into the pot. The old man then asks for salt and pepper, and begins to stir the soup in the village square. He announces that these stones will make good soup, but it would be much better if there were some carrots. Someone runs and brings carrots, then cabbage is called for and found. As the soup is stirred someone mentions that the soup would be even better with a bit of beef, and a few potatoes, and some barley and milk, all of which are added. Finally the soup was ready. Never had there been such a feast. Never had the peasants tasted such soup! And to think it was made from stones!!! The pebble soup story is not completely nonsense. The late great chef Alexandre Dumaine always put pebbles into his court bouillon so that all the ingredients would be well covered with the liquid and the soup would be strong!

According to *Larousse Gastronomique*, in the 17th century, the word potage did not have the same meaning as it has today–this name was given to great big dishes of meat or fish boiled with vegetables. Grimod de la Reynière said of soup:

"It is to a dinner what a portico or a peristyle is to a building; that is to say, it is not only the first part of it, but must be devised in such a manner as the overture of an opera announces the subject of the work." At ceremonial dinners, the menu often includes two soups, a clear and a thick one. Depending on their consistency, soups can then be classified into two main categories: clear soups and thick soups. (A clear soup is a consommé with various light garnishes added.) Originally soup was basic sustenance–a dish of warm nourishment that was a meal in itself. Cockaleekie is a well known Scottish soup made with an old cock, leeks, (hence the name) and seasonings. Gazpacho is more or less new to the American menu, but it was made as far back as Mary Randolph's time, and in her book, *The Virginia Housewife*, (1800s) she designated it as a salad. It is a cold soup of Spanish origin, made with fresh tomatoes, oil, seasonings, and garnished with diced fresh tomatoes, green peppers, cucumbers, chopped chives, and croutons. The variations on the recipe are almost endless. In the US, chopped eggs are frequently added as garnish. Alexander Dumas had two favorite ladies: Mademoiselle Mars and Mademoiselle George, who both set a "gourmet table." Mademoiselle Mars's housekeeper-cook served her a Soupe aux amandes, by blanching the almonds and removing the skins. Then the almonds were pounded and crushed in a mortar. Just before the guests went to the table, she poured boiling water over that very smooth paste, strained it all through a very fine cloth and added hot milk to it.

Stew on the other hand, is from Middle English or French (dating around 1300-1475) meaning a hot broth or fish or meat usually with vegetables prepared by stewing (to boil) slowly or with simmering heat. In stewing, the meat is usually cubed and browned in hot fat. Vegetables, onions, and seasonings are added, with enough liquid to cover the basic ingredients. The stew is then cooked in a covered pot on top of the stove or in a 350° F. oven. The cooking liquid may be thickened into a sauce at the beginning or end of the recipe. Recommended cuts of beef for stews include: top round, bottom round, and chuck steak. These are considered the best selections as they do not have a lot of fat, are fibrous, and tough. During cooking, the fibers are broken down and tenderized. Other meats such as lamb, veal, chicken or fish may be used, but chicken and fish will require less cooking time.

Stewing is very similar to braising. In stewing you will need about 3/4 cup of liquid for each pound of uncooked meat, chicken, or fish. The amount of liquid needed for a vegetable stew will vary because of the amount of water in the vegetables themselves. The preparation of a stew is similar to the preparation of a soup. The difference being that less liquid is used, and the cooking time is longer. If you have a freezer, it is worth doubling the recipe when preparing a stew since it freezes well, and it does not take any longer to make a stew for 12 than for 6. Remember to chill the stew and remove the fat before freezing (be sure the stew is at room temperature before freezing or ice crystals will form and your stew will be mushy). To serve frozen stew, thaw in the refrigerator, then reheat.

Essential Soup Tools

Soup preparation is easy with a few good tools. Included should be a big heavy kettle that holds at least 4 quarts or more of liquid and has a tight fitting lid; a stockpot that is bigger than a soup kettle and holds at least 6 quarts of liquid; a 4-quart size Dutch oven; a food processor or blender; a collection of wooden spoons; a skimmer; a ladle; a strainer; good knives for cutting, dicing, and chopping; a sauté pan; if you have either a pressure cooker or electric crockpot (slow cooker) you have

almost everything you could need. Old-fashioned pressure cooking has 3 main benefits for the modern cook: one pot convenience, versatility of foods that can be prepared, and speed.

The pressure cooker can be used to make stocks and broths very quickly (from 30 minutes to an hour from beginning to end) but soup made in a pressure cooker produces a soup that is different in taste from the same soup prepared in a slow cooker! This has to do with the boiling action of the pots, since steam cannot escape from a slow cooker. The pressure cooker, which can be electric or stovetop is available in a 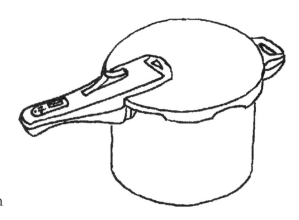 variety of sizes and is very safe and easy to use. The concept is simple. By securing the lid of the pot, water or other liquid can be heated to higher temperatures than can be attained under normal cooking conditions. Foods are then cooked in this super-heated atmosphere.

When used for preparing soups, the pressure cooker has two specific talents: blending the flavor of several vegetables in a stock, and breaking down the vegetable fibers quickly and uniformly to create a silky smooth purée. The pressure cooker can also save a tremendous amount of time. Pressure cookers are very easy and safe to use once you understand the simple techniques. Just remember that when cooking in a pressure cooker, do not fill it more than 2/3 full when preparing soups.

Essential Hints:

The fresher and finer the ingredients, the better the soup or stew.

Preparing soups and stews the day before, and refrigerating overnight, allows the flavors to intensify. If you make soup the day before serving, and refrigerate, the fat will congeal at the top and can be easily skimmed off.

Freeze any leftover chicken and meat bones for use in soups and stocks.

Don't peel vegetables for broths as they improve color and flavor.

Buy older meats and fowl for making broths as they have more flavor.

There are 2 kinds of canned, ready to serve broth, but while one needs no diluting, the other (condensed) requires water or milk to be added.

If you keep your canned broth in the refrigerator, the fat will congeal at the top and can be skimmed off before using.

For maximum flavor when preparing soups, place the soup bones in the liquid base before you begin heating it.

The cooking liquid from vegetables or meats can be frozen and used as a nutritious base for soups or stews.

Stock can easily be clarified by adding shells from 2 to 3 eggs and simmering for about 10 minutes before straining out the shells and adding other ingredients.

Finely chopped meats and vegetables in soups enables them to cook much faster than large pieces.

Stews can be cooked in a 350° F. oven as well as on top of the stove.

Add sour cream or yogurt to hot soup without letting it come to a boil. Heat it gently on low until the mixture is warmed through. Boiling will cause curdling.

If your soup curdles, strain it, then place in a blender or food processor, and process until smooth. Remember not to fill the container more than 2/3 full, and blend on low speed, then increase to high.

Adding chicken or beef bouillon cubes or powder to your soups will intensify the flavor of the soup. Never add salt, pepper, or seasonings until you are almost through cooking your stew or soup. If your soup is too salty, add a peeled, thinly sliced raw potato and simmer for about 10-15 minutes. Remove potato and serve.

The first step in making many soups is to sauté the onions, which form the flavor base of all types of soups. Then you usually add the liquid; simmer, thicken, blend, then garnish.

How quickly soups cook makes a big difference. The cooking period is usually long, and you can add more liquid if the water gets below the solid ingredients.

Simmer means slowest bubbling possible; next comes slow boil (a little faster); then boil, and the fastest, rapid boil: where you cook as quickly as possible.

When puréeing soups in a food processor or blender, purée only 2 cups at a time, and when using hot liquids and ingredients, leave off the removable cap from the center of the lid so the steam can escape.

Taste the soup often to achieve the right flavor, but let the soup cool in the spoon before tasting it to get the real flavor.

A 5-pound pumpkin will yield about 4 cups of purée. If stored in a cool, dry place, pumpkins can keep for several weeks. Cut and wrapped in plastic, you can refrigerate them for up to 5 days. Once they are cooked and puréed, you can freeze them for almost a year.

Aromatic vegetables like onions or turnips give flavor to a stock for hours, but small fresh garden vegetables will not remain crisp if cooked too long in the soup.

If you don't have any fish stock, a combination of bottled clam juice and white wine will do.

Make sure the containers used for soups and stews are large and have a tight fitting lid.

While cooking meats, be very careful not to pierce them with a fork or the necessary juices will escape.

Many spices and flavorings will vary in intensity, especially curry powder and soy sauces, so taste as you go.

Fresh herbs are not as strong as dried ones. It takes 1/2 teaspoon of a dried herb to replace a tablespoon of a fresh one.

When freezing soups and stews, be careful not to overcook them since they will have additional cooking time when reheated. Shorten specified cooking times by 10 minutes if you are going to freeze them.

To peel a tomato easily, spear it with a kitchen fork, then plunge it in boiling water for 30 seconds. Remove from the water, and the skin will slide right off.

In general, a pinch refers to dried seasonings, and a dash refers to liquid ingredients (Worcestershire, Tabasco). Occasionally a recipe will call for a dash of salt or pepper but do not go overboard.

There are several ways to thicken a soup, such as adding a starch like flour, cornstarch, potatoes, rice, or beans. Another way is to thicken soup is by puréeing it in the blender or food processor. Soup can be thickened if it is boiled to reduce the amount of liquid, and some soups are thickened by adding egg yolks.

One tablespoon of cornstarch stirred into two tablespoons of cold water and added to one cup of boiling liquid will also serve to thicken a soup. This mixture is always added just before serving the soup. If you add it at the beginning, the cornstarch will break down and the liquid will thin out again. If you want to add long grain rice, one cup will absorb about three cups of water, and must be added in the final twenty minutes of cooking.

One tablespoon of flour combined with one tablespoon of melted butter or heated oil, can be stirred into four cups of liquid to form the base for a soup.

Add beans in the beginning of the soup preparation since they require a longer time to cook.

For six cups of soup, beat two egg yolks lightly and add two tablespoons of heavy cream. Then carefully add 1/4 cup of hot soup to the egg/cream mixture, stirring well. (This heats the egg yolk slightly and should prevent curdling.) Stirring well, return this mixture to the soup. Do not let the soup return to a boil or it will curdle.

An easy way to thicken vegetable or other soups is with a vegetable purée. To prepare: cook extra vegetables, remove them from the soup with a slotted spoon, and purée them in a blender or processor with a little liquid. Then stir the purée back into the soup.

Chilling soups will tone down the flavor, so taste it before serving, and adjust the seasoning if needed.

Cold soups will be thicker after chilling.

Garnishing soups make them look more appealing, and can contribute to the flavor. Easy garnishes include finely chopped scallion greens, finely chopped chives, a spoonful of sour cream, minced parsley or basil, or croutons. Another great garnish is grated cheese.

JEFFERSON'S PIGEON SOUP

© *Cuisine Magazine* by Bert Greene, 1984; *Jefferson the Great Gastronome*, page 64. The following recipe was reconstructed for contemporary kitchens using ingredients from Jefferson's journals, his daughter Martha Randolph's receipt books, and from the *Thomas Jefferson Cookbook*, by the late
Marie Fiske Kimball.

INGREDIENTS

2 tablespoons of unsalted butter
2 small pigeons or Rock Cornish hens, split down the back (1 pound each)
2 large parsnips, pared and chopped
2 large carrots, pared and chopped
2 medium leeks, trimmed, rinsed, cut crosswise into 1/2-inch pieces
2 medium ribs of celery, trimmed and chopped
pinch of dried thyme, crumbled
6 cups of Chicken Stock or Chicken Broth (see recipe on page 88)
2 cups of heavy cream
1/2 cup of fine, fresh soft bread crumbs
1/2 cup of shredded fresh spinach, rinsed and drained
1 tablespoon of chopped fresh parsley
1 teaspoon of salt
dash of ground mace
freshly ground pepper

SERVES 6

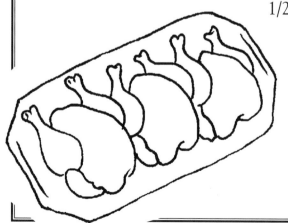

(1) Melt butter in a large, heavy saucepan over medium heat. Add pigeons, skin side down; sauté until lightly browned, about 5 minutes.

(2) Scatter parsnips, carrots, leeks, and celery over pigeons; sprinkle with thyme. Reduce heat to low; cook, covered, until pigeons and vegetables are tender, about 1 hour.

(3) Add chicken stock to saucepan; increase heat to medium. Heat to boiling, then reduce heat to low; simmer, covered, until pigeons are very tender, about 30 minutes.

(4) Remove saucepan from heat. Transfer pigeons to plate; let stand until cool enough to handle. Strain stock through sieve into a heat-proof bowl, pressing vegetables in sieve with back of spoon to extract as much flavor as possible; discard contents of sieve. Return stock to saucepan.

(5) Stir cream and bread crumbs in medium bowl until smooth; stir into stock in saucepan. Heat to boiling, then reduce heat to low; simmer, uncovered, 5 minutes. Add spinach and parsley, simmer uncovered, about 5 minutes longer.

(6) Remove pigeon meat from bones; remove and discard skin. Tear meat into bite-sized pieces; sprinkle with salt, mace, and pepper to taste. Stir meat into soup; cook until heated through, about 5 minutes. Ladle into warmed soup bowls. Serve immediately.

Thomas Jefferson's formal dining room at Monticello.

AVOCADO VELVET SOUP

(1) Cut the avocados in half, peel them, and remove the seeds.
(2) Cut the avocados into small pieces.
(3) Place the avocado pieces in a food processor or blender and process or blend until very smooth.
(4) Add the chicken broth, sour cream, water, lime juice, salt, pepper, and onion salt. Blend until smooth.
(5) Chill well until serving.

NOTE: A velvety smooth soup that can be served as a light summer lunch or as the prelude to an elegant dinner.

 INGREDIENTS

2 ripe avocados
1 3/4 cups of chicken broth
1 cup of sour cream
1/2 cup of water
2 teaspoons of lime juice
dash of salt
freshly ground pepper
1/4 teaspoon of onion salt

SERVES 4

ICED TOMATO SOUP

(1) Place tomatoes, onion, water, pepper and salt in a pot.
(2) Bring the water to a boil and cook briskly for about 6 or 7 minutes.
(3) Stir in the tomato paste and mix well.
(4) Mix the flour with a little bit of cold water to form a paste; then whisk this mixture into the soup. Blend well.
(5) Add the hot chicken broth and continue stirring until the soup comes to a boil.
(6) Remove soup from the heat and press the soup through a fine sieve, using a wooden spoon to force as much of the vegetable pulp through as possible.
(7) Stir the soup for a few minutes and then let it cool.
(8) When soup is cool, stir in the cream and taste the soup to see if it needs more salt or pepper.
(9) Serve soup in glasses or bowls and sprinkle each portion with the dill before serving. This may be made a few days ahead. Serve cold.

 INGREDIENTS

6 ripe tomatoes, coarsely chopped
1 onion, chopped
1/4 cup of water
freshly ground pepper
pinch of salt
2 tablespoons of tomato paste
2 tablespoons of flour
2 cups of hot chicken broth
1 cup of whipping cream or heavy cream
chopped dill or dill weed

NOTE: *A delight on a hot evening, this does not have a strong tomato taste but is very rich.*

SERVES 4

COLD CHERRY SOUP

(1) In a large pan, combine the water, sugar and cinnamon.

(2) Bring to a boil and add the cherries.

(3) Partially cover the pan and simmer over low heat for 10 minutes.

(4) Combine the cornstarch with 2 tablespoons of cold water and stir into the soup. Stirring constantly, bring the soup almost to a boil.

(5) Reduce the heat and simmer about 2 minutes or until it is clear and slightly thickened.

(6) Pour soup into a shallow bowl (to chill faster) and place in the refrigerator until chilled.

(7) Before serving, chill the bowls you will serve the soup in, and stir in the cream and the wine.

NOTE: This is so sweet you could use it for a dessert.

 INGREDIENTS

3 cups of cold water
1 cup of sugar
1/2 teaspoon of cinnamon
4 cups of sour (tart) cherries, pitted and drained
1 tablespoon of cornstarch
1/4 cup of whipping cream, chilled
3/4 cup of dry red wine, chilled (a Beaujolais is good)

SERVES 4-6

CANTALOUPE SOUP

(1) Place the cubes of cantaloupe in a food processor or blender container.
(2) Add the champagne, sugar, and lime juice; then blend until smooth or slightly lumpy.
(3) Pour the soup into a serving bowl and refrigerate, covered, for at least 3 hours.
(4) To serve, spoon the soup into individual cups and garnish with mint leaves.

NOTE: Cantaloupe is one of the most nutritious and low-calorie fruits available. When you tire of serving it plain or in salads, here is a different way to use it.

 INGREDIENTS

3 pounds of cantaloupe, peeled, seeded, and cut into 1-inch cubes
1/2 cup of champagne (or ginger ale) or more
2 tablespoons of sugar
1 tablespoon of lime juice
mint leaves for garnish

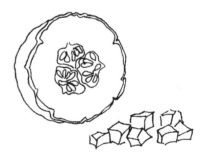

SERVES 4-6

AMBROSIA

(1) Place the orange juice in a large, heavy kettle over medium heat.
(2) Grate the reserved orange peel and add it to the juice.
(3) Peel any remaining white skin or membrane from the oranges, and place the orange sections in a blender or food processor; lightly chop them and add them to the kettle.
(4) Add the cinnamon stick, rum, sherry, sugar, and cloves to the soup and bring to a boil.
(5) Add the coconut, pineapple, and almonds.
(6) Reduce heat and simmer, stirring occasionally, for 15 minutes.
(7) Stir in the sour cream and chill the soup well before serving.

NOTE: One of my favorite cold soups, from a café in Philadelphia.

 INGREDIENTS

1/2 gallon of orange juice
6 oranges, peeled (reserve peel)
1 cinnamon stick
1 1/2 cups of dark rum
1/2 cup of dry sherry
1/2 to 1 cup of superfine sugar
1/2 teaspoon of ground cloves
2 cups of shredded coconut
1 fresh pineapple, cubed
1/2 cup of ground almonds
4 cups of sour cream

SERVES 20

GAZPACHO

(1) Several hours before serving, combine 2 of the chopped tomatoes, half the cucumber, and half the onion with the chopped green pepper in a large bowl.

(2) Add about 3/4 cup of the tomato juice.

(3) Place 1/2 of the mixture in a blender container and blend at high speed for 1 minute to purée the vegetables.

(4) Repeat with the other half. Return the puréed mixture to the bowl, and, using a wire whisk, mix the purée with the remaining tomato juice, 9 tablespoons of olive oil, the vinegar, Tabasco sauce, salt and pepper.

(5) Refrigerate this mixture, covered, until well chilled–at least 3 hours.

(6) In a small skillet, heat the remaining 2 tablespoons of olive oil over medium low heat.

(7) Sauté the garlic and bread cubes until crisp and golden.

(8) Drain the bread cubes well on a paper towel.

(9) Set the garlic aside to cool. Crush the cooled garlic and add to the chilled soup.

(10) To serve, ladle the chilled soup into a tureen.

(11) Arrange the reserved chopped vegetables and the croutons in small bowls and serve along with the soup to be sprinkled on top of each serving.

NOTE: Chopped, hard boiled eggs can also be used as a garnish.

NOTE: A cold soup of Spanish origin that is ideal for warm weather entertaining.

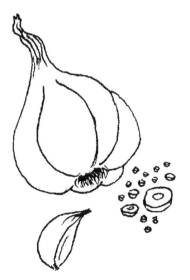

 INGREDIENTS

3 tomatoes, peeled and chopped
1 large cucumber, peeled and
    chopped
1 large onion, finely chopped
1 green pepper, seeded and
    chopped
2 1/2 cups of tomato juice
11 tablespoons of olive oil
7 tablespoons of red wine vinegar
dash of Tabasco sauce
pinch of salt
freshly ground pepper
3 cloves of garlic, peeled and
    halved
3 thinly sliced pieces of white
    bread with their crusts
    removed, cut into cubes

SERVES 6

BLUEBERRY SOUP

(1) In a medium-sized pot, combine 2 cups of the blueberries with the lemon juice.

(2) Simmer for a few minutes, stirring, until the blueberries begin to give off their juice.

(3) Place berry mixture in a food processor or blender and purée.

(4) Combine the sugar, cornstarch, and cinnamon in the pot.

(5) Stir in the cranbury juice and cook over low to medium heat until sauce is smooth and well blended.

(6) Place a fine mesh colander or sieve over the pot, and with the back of a wooden spoon, press the puréed blueberry mixture through the wire and into the pot.

(7) Throw away pulp and seeds of the blueberries.

(8) Add the wine and the lemon slice to the soup.

(9) Bring soup to a boil, stirring constantly.

(10) Reduce heat to simmer, and cook for another minute or two, stirring, until soup begins to thicken and becomes clear.

(11) Remove pot from heat and stir in vanilla. Taste soup for sweetness, adding more sugar if necessary.

(12) Refrigerate soup until cool.

(13) Remove lemon slice and stir in remaining berries.

(14) Cover and chill, overnight if possible, before serving.

NOTE: *To serve, after spooning into soup bowls, add a large dollop of one of the garnishes.*

INGREDIENTS

4 cups of fresh blueberries,
  divided
1/4 cup of fresh lemon juice
1/2 cup (or more) of sugar
2 tablespoons of cornstarch
pinch of cinnamon
1 cup of cranberry juice cocktail
1/2 cup of dry white wine
1/2 thick slice of lemon, without seeds
1 teaspoon of vanilla

Cool Whip, yogurt, or whipped
  cream (optional)

SERVES 4

THE BEST ONION SOUP EVER

(1) In a large skillet, melt the butter, add the onion slices, separating the rings with a fork.

(2) Cook, stirring, until all the rings are coated with butter. Continue cooking until the onions are soft and golden brown.

(3) Sprinkle the flour, salt and pepper to taste, and a pinch of cayenne pepper over the onions, and cook for 2 to 3 minutes, stirring constantly, until the flour browns lightly.

(4) Meanwhile, in a small saucepan, heat the broth to a boil and add to the onions.

(5) Bring the mixture to a boil; lower the heat, and simmer 15 minutes.

NOTE: *At this point, the mixture may be made in advance and refrigerated.*

(6) About 20 minutes before serving, transfer the onion soup to a large kettle and add the champagne. A whole bottle of champagne will produce a thin soup, if you desire a thicker consistency, use less champagne. Stir well to blend, and simmer over low heat.

(7) Arrange the bread slices on an ungreased cookie sheet and bake at 250° F. until they are crisp and lightly browned, turning once.

(8) Arrange the bread slices in the bottom of a large casserole in one or two layers.

(9) Sprinkle half of the grated cheese over the bread.

(10) Pour the soup over the bread, and cover with the remaining grated cheese.

(11) Broil 6 inches from the heat, just long enough to melt the cheese and brown the top lightly.

(12) Serve immediately.

NOTE: *Here the lowly onion is transformed into a grand gastronomic experience! Serve before a light main course, or as a late evening meal in itself.*

 INGREDIENTS

1/4 pound of butter
1 pound of Spanish onions, very
  thinly sliced
1 heaping tablespoon of flour
pinch of salt
freshly ground pepper
pinch of cayenne pepper
3 cups of chicken broth
1 fifth of good champagne, well
  chilled
10 thin slices of day-old French
  bread
1 cup of grated, Gruyère cheese

SERVES 6-8

PEANUT SOUP

(1) In a large saucepan, over medium heat, melt the butter.

(2) Stir in the celery and the scallions and cook until translucent.

(3) Stir in the flour, and stir constantly for a few minutes. Do not let flour burn or get dark brown as it will ruin the soup.

(4) Gradually stir in the stock and milk, stirring constantly until the mixture is thick and smooth.

(5) Strain the mixture, cool for a few minutes, and purée in a blender or food processor.

(6) Return the purée to the liquid.

(7) Add the peanut butter, and mix well, using a whisk or egg beater until mixture is smooth.

(8) Season to taste with Tabasco and salt.

(9) Bring the soup to serving temperature. Do not allow to boil. Garnish if desired with chopped peanuts or chopped chives.

 INGREDIENTS

2 tablespoons of butter
1 rib of celery, chopped fine
5 scallions, trimmed and sliced thin, with as much green as possible
3 tablespoons of flour
2 cups of chicken stock or broth (see page 88)
2 cups of milk
1/2 cup of smooth or chunky peanut butter
a few drops of Tabasco
pinch of salt

chopped peanuts; chopped chives (optional)

SERVES 4-6

RENÉE'S SWEET & SOUR CABBAGE SOUP

(1) Place the meat in a large kettle with the water and bring to a boil; skim off fat as it rises. This takes about 5-10 minutes.

(2) When broth is clear, add cabbage and reduce heat to medium.

(3) Add onion and tomatoes, cover and cook for 2 hours or more (you can cook this much longer for 4 hours or so on low heat, adding more water if necessary).

(4) Squeeze in the juice of two lemons, the sugar, salt, and pepper.

(5) Cook another 30 minutes and taste to see if more lemon juice or sugar is needed.

(6) Cool soup before refrigerating, and skim off fat before reheating.

NOTE: *Great served with pumpernickel bread that has been rubbed with fresh garlic!*

 INGREDIENTS

1-1 1/2 pounds of short ribs or Flanken, with or without bones (bones make it better), cut into pieces

8 cups of water (or more)

1 head of cabbage, shredded

1 large onion, peeled

28 ounces of whole, peeled, tomatoes

juice of 2-4 lemons

1/4 cup (or more) of dark brown sugar

pinch of salt

freshly ground pepper

SERVES 8

TURKEY SOUP

(1) In a large pot, combine the turkey carcass, garlic, onion, bay leaves, sage, Worcestershire sauce, sugar, salt, and water.

(2) Bring the mixture to a boil; reduce heat, and simmer, covered for about 1 1/2 hours, or until the meat falls from the bones.

(3) Remove the turkey carcass. Cut any remaining meat from the bones and cut meat into small pieces. Set aside the meat and discard the carcass and bones.

(4) Strain the broth, and let it cool.

(5) Refrigerate the broth and the meat overnight, if possible, and remove any fat from the soup.

(6) Add the carrots, celery, and corn to the broth, and bring the broth to a boil.

(7) Reduce the heat and simmer, covered, for about 45 minutes or until the vegetables are tender.

(8) Stir in the reserved turkey meat and season with salt, pepper, and parsley to taste.

INGREDIENTS

1 leftover turkey carcass, broken, plus
      any meat on it (I use the carcass
      from a 5-6 pound turkey breast but
      a whole carcass can be used.)
3 garlic cloves, peeled and chopped
2 onions, peeled and chopped
2 bay leaves
1 teaspoon of sage
1 tablespoon of Worcestershire sauce
2 teaspoons of sugar
1 tablespoon of salt
8 cups of water
3 carrots, peeled and cut into 1/2-
      inch rounds
3 ribs of celery, chopped
10 ounces of frozen corn, thawed to
      room temperature
reserved turkey meat
salt to taste
freshly ground pepper
2 tablespoons of chopped parsley

SERVES 8-10

PUMPKIN APPLE SOUP

(1) In a large pot, over medium low heat, melt the butter, and sauté the onion until soft, about 5 minutes.

(2) Add the chicken stock, apples, pumpkin purée, salt, sugar, and nutmeg.

(3) Stir to mix well. Slowly bring the mixture to the boil, reduce heat; cover and simmer, stirring occasionally, until apples are tender, about 20-30 minutes.

(4) Remove the apples and onions, and purée in a blender or food processor. Return to liquid in pot and stir in the milk, cream, cinnamon, and curry.

(5) Simmer another 5 to 10 minutes, and add brandy and pepper.

(6) Simmer another 5 minutes and serve.

To prepare fresh pumpkin:

(1) Wash and cut the pumpkin in half crosswise.

(2) Remove the seeds and strings, and place it in the oven, side up.

(3) Bake at 325° F. for 1 hour or more, depending on the size of the pumpkin or until pumpkin is tender and begins to fall apart.

(4) Scrape the pulp from the shell and push through a ricer or strainer.

NOTE: A puréed soup for a cold winter's night. For added flavor, top with freshly grated Gruyère cheese.

INGREDIENTS

1 tablespoon of unsalted butter
1/2 cup of onion, chopped
2 1/2-3 cups of chicken stock (see
    page 88)
2 tart apples, peeled, cored, seeded,
    chopped and tossed with 1 tea-
    spoon of lemon juice
1-1 1/2 cups of pumpkin purée (see
    note to prepare fresh pumpkin
    on page 36)
1 teaspoon of salt
1 teaspoon of brown sugar
1/2 teaspoon of freshly grated nutmeg
3/4 cup of milk
1/4 cup of heavy cream
1 teaspoon of cinnamon
1 teaspoon of curry
2 tablespoons of brandy
freshly ground white pepper

SERVES 4-6

LENTIL SOUP WITH BRIE

(1) Rinse the lentils well in a colander, under running warm water.

(2) Place lentils in a pot with 1 1/2 quarts of water. Bring to a boil; remove from heat, cover, and let stand until lentils are soft (anywhere from 1 to 4 hours). Do not discard the water.

(3) In a small pan, melt the butter and sauté the onion until transparent. Do not brown.

(4) Combine tomatoes, carrots, celery, garlic, chicken broth, beef broth, Worcestershire sauce, vinegar, pepper, thyme, and bay leaf in a large pot. Be sure to add the water from the soaking lentils.

(5) Simmer over low heat, uncovered, for about 45 minutes.

(6) Remove the bay leaf, and discard.

(7) Scoop out the vegetables from the soup and purée in a blender or food processor until chunky, removing the tube from the food processor lid to let the steam out.

(8) Return vegetables to broth and add salt.

NOTE: *The soup may be frozen at this point.*

(9) Before serving, place a piece of cheese in the bottom of each bowl.

(10) Heat soup to piping hot and ladle it over the cheese.

(11) Garnish with parsley if desired.

INGREDIENTS

1 cup of dried lentils
1 tablespoon of butter
l onion, finely chopped
4 tomatoes, peeled and chopped
3-4 carrots, peeled and chopped
3 ribs of celery, chopped
3 cloves of garlic, minced
2 1/2 cups of chicken broth
l cup of beef broth
1 1/2 tablespoons of Worcestershire
    sauce
1 tablespoon of cider vinegar
freshly ground pepper
1/2 teaspoon of dried thyme
l bay leaf
pinch of salt
6 l/2-ounce pieces of Brie cheese

freshly chopped parsley (optional)

SERVES 6

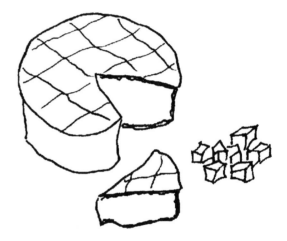

SEAFOOD AND CHICKEN GUMBO

(1) In a large pot, brown the chicken in 3 tablespoons of butter.
(2) Remove chicken from the pot. If no butter is left, melt another 3 tablespoons of butter.
(3) Whisk in the flour to make a roux, stirring until golden brown. Do not let flour burn.
(4) Add the onion, celery, pepper and garlic. Cook until wilted.
(5) Return chicken to the pot and add 2 quarts of water, tomato, and the bay leaf. Simmer for 30 minutes.
(6) In a medium-sized saucepan, fry the okra in the vegetable oil. Cook until slightly browned. Add more oil if needed. Drain well on paper towel.
(7) Add okra, crab halves, and shrimp to the gumbo.
(8) Simmer 20-30 minutes in a covered pot.
(9) Add salt, pepper to taste.
(10) Serve over rice.

 INGREDIENTS

3-4 pound chicken (fryer), cut into chunks
6 tablespoons of butter
3 tablespoons of flour
1 large onion, chopped
2 ribs of celery, chopped
1/4 cup of chopped, green pepper
1 garlic clove, chopped
2 quarts of water
1 tomato, chopped
1 bay leaf
1 pound okra, sliced
1/4 cup of vegetable oil
6 cleaned crabs, halved
1 pound of large shrimp
pinch of salt
freshly ground pepper

SERVES 4

DILL PICKLE SOUP

(1) In a large kettle, combine the chicken broth, bouillon, carrots, potatoes, and celery. Bring to a boil, cover; then reduce heat and simmer gently for 10 minutes. Do not overcook.

(2) Add pickles and cook another 15 minutes.

(3) In a small bowl, whisk milk and flour together until smooth.

(4) Whisk in a small amount of hot soup and return mixture to soup pot, blending well.

(5) Return soup to a boil, stirring until slightly thickened.

(6) Remove from heat.

(7) In a small bowl, whisk egg with sour cream and whisk in a small amount of hot soup. Blend well, and return to pot; heat and stir until smooth. Do not boil.

(8) Keep warm, and if reheating do not let boil.

(9) Season with the pepper, garnish, and serve.

INGREDIENTS

8 cups of chicken broth
2 chicken bouillon cubes or 2-teaspoons of chicken soup base or stock (see page 88)
2 carrots, coarsely grated (you can use the food processor)
2 cups of peeled and diced potatoes
1 cup of thinly sliced celery
6 coarsely grated, Polish dill pickles (you can use the processor)
1/2 cup of milk
3 tablespoons of flour
1 egg
5 tablespoons of sour cream
freshly ground pepper
finely chopped parsley or dill for garnish

SERVES 10

LEMON GRASS AND
CUCUMBER SOUP

(1) In a medium saucepan, heat the chicken broth and lemon grass. Bring to a boil.
(2) Reduce heat and simmer soup for 15 minutes.
(3) Stir in the cucumber and simmer another 4-5 minutes.
(4) Remove soup from the heat and discard lemon grass.
(5) Ladle the soup into bowls and garnish with the cilantro.

NOTE: *When using fresh lemon grass, remove any of the dried outer leaves. Tie the stalks together with a piece of thread. If using dried lemon grass, place them in a double thickness of cheesecloth.*

 INGREDIENTS

5 stalks of fresh or 1/4 cup dried lemon grass, sliced or shredded (see note)
4-5 cups of chicken broth
1/4 medium cucumber, halved lengthwise, peeled, seeded, and sliced into 1/8-inch slices
2-3 tablespoons of chopped cilantro for garnish

SERVES 4

BOSTON CARROT SOUP

(1) Boil carrots in a heavy pot with water and chicken bouillon cube, sugar, and butter, for a few minutes.
(2) Remove carrots from broth and purée in food processor. Set aside.
(3) Add cream to the broth and bring soup to a boil.
(4) Reduce heat to simmer, add carrot purée, and stir well to blend.
(5) Add pepper, and taste to see if salt is needed.

 INGREDIENTS

2 pounds of carrots, peeled and cut into small chunks
6 cups of water
1 chicken bouillon cube
1/4 cup of sugar
1/4 pound of butter
6 cups of heavy cream
freshly ground pepper
salt to taste

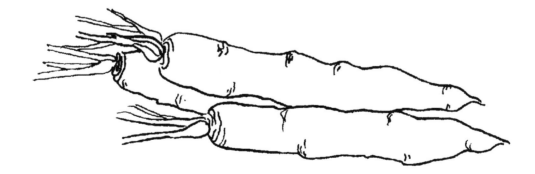

SERVES 6

SPINACH EGG DROP SOUP

(1) In a large saucepan, bring 1 cup of the chicken broth to a boil and add the spinach.

(2) Cover the saucepan and cook over high heat until the spinach is bright green and well cooked.

(3) With a slotted spoon, remove the spinach from the broth and set aside.

(4) Add the remaining broth to the saucepan, and bring to a boil.

(5) In a small bowl, beat the egg lightly, then beat in the grated cheese.

(6) When the broth is boiling, pour in the egg-cheese mixture, stirring constantly.

(7) Add the spinach and pepper. Cook for another minute and serve immediately.

NOTE: Also called stracciatella or Rags Soup.

 INGREDIENTS

3 1/2 cups of chicken broth
10 ounces of frozen, chopped spinach
1 egg
1/4 cup of freshly grated Parmesan cheese
freshly ground pepper

SERVES 6-8

LEMON SOUP

(1) In a medium saucepan over medium heat, cook the broth and the rice for 15 to 20 minutes.
(2) In a small bowl, beat the eggs lightly, and gradually add the lemon juice, beating continuously.
(3) Pour a small amount of the hot soup into the egg mixture; then return this mixture to the soup in the saucepan. Do not heat any further. If the eggs begin to curdle, beat the soup with a wire whisk.
(4) Serve at once.

NOTE: Easy and impressive.

 INGREDIENTS

6 cups of chicken broth
3 tablespoons of uncooked, long grain, white rice
3 eggs
3 tablespoons of lemon juice

SERVES 4-6

EGGPLANT SOUP

(1) In a large skillet, heat the oil over medium high heat, and sauté the eggplant cubes until they are light brown.

(2) Remove the eggplant from the skillet and set aside.

(3) In the same skillet, sauté the scallions and garlic, adding a little more oil if necessary.

(4) Stir in the flour and the curry powder with a wire whisk, blending well.

(5) Add the chicken broth, rosemary, marjoram, salt and pepper to taste; mix well.

(6) Add the eggplant cubes and cook over medium heat for 30 minutes.

(7) Stir in the cream and heat slightly; do not overheat or the soup will curdle.

(8) Serve immediately.

NOTE: *This soup can also be frozen and reheated.*

 INGREDIENTS

1/2 cup of vegetable oil
2 pounds of eggplant, peeled and cubed
2 bunches of scallions, chopped
3 garlic cloves, crushed
1/4 cup of flour
1 tablespoon of curry powder
5 cups of chicken broth
1 teaspoon of rosemary
1 teaspoon of marjoram
pinch of salt
freshly ground pepper
1 1/4 cups of whipping cream

SERVES 4-6

BEER SOUP

(1) Over low heat, combine the beer and sugar, stirring constantly.
(2) Place milk and cinnamon in another pan and heat on low. Do not boil.
(3) In a bowl, beat together the eggs, sour cream, and nutmeg.
(4) Add the hot beer mixture, beating well.
(5) Beat in the milk and cinnamon.
(6) Pour the soup into a heavy saucepan and heat well, stirring constantly.

NOTE: *Do not let the soup boil.*

 INGREDIENTS

2 12-ounce cans of beer
6 tablespoons of sugar
1 cup of milk
1/8 teaspoon of ground cinnamon
2 eggs
1/2 cup of sour cream
freshly grated nutmeg

SERVES 4-6

PURÉED VEGETABLE SOUP

(1) In a large pot, combine the parsnips, carrots, celery, turnip, onions, and broth.
(2) Bring to a boil, reduce heat, cover and simmer for about 50 minutes or until vegetables are very tender.
(3) Remove from heat and let soup cool a little.
(4) Remove tube from processor lid.
(5) In a food processor fitted with the steel blade, purée the mixture in batches.
(6) Add boiling water, if necessary, to thin soup to the desired consistency.
(7) Season with salt and fresh ground pepper.
(8) Ladle soup into bowl, each containing a tablespoon of sour cream, if desired.
(9) Garnish and serve.

NOTE: Simple, easy, and nourishing. Given to me by a student while teaching a cooking class.

 INGREDIENTS

1 pound of parsnips, chopped
1/2 pound of carrots, peeled and chopped
2 ribs of celery, sliced on the diagonal (prevents strings)
1 small turnip, peeled and chopped
2 onions, peeled and chopped
3 1/2 cups of chicken broth
6 tablespoons of sour cream
pinch of salt
freshly ground pepper

croutons and chopped fresh parsley (optional)

SERVES 6

REBA'S CHICKEN SOUP

(1) Place chicken in a large pot and cover with enough cold water to cover chicken plus 1 inch.

(2) Bring to a boil. Skim off bubbles and residue.

(3) Add onion, carrots, celery, and parsley.

(4) Stir in bouillon cubes or powder.

(5) Lower heat to simmer, cover, and cook until chicken is done, about 45 minutes.

(6) Remove chicken and let soup cool.

(7) Strain broth. Keep chicken separate and tear before adding to soup and serving.

(8) Add salt and pepper to taste.

NOTE: May be frozen.

 INGREDIENTS

4-7 half breasts or whole chicken, cleaned
whole onion, peeled
4-6 carrots, peeled
3 ribs of celery with tops, cut in chunks
3 tablespoons of fresh parsley
3 chicken bouillon cubes or 3 tablespoons of packaged powder
pinch of salt
freshly ground pepper

SERVES 6-8

CREAM OF ALMOND SOUP

(1) Place the flour, butter, and potato starch in a large bowl.

(2) Cream until the flour and potato starch are thoroughly incorporated into the butter. Form into a ball, and set the bowl aside.

(3) Heat the chicken broth in a medium saucepan.

(4) Add 1 cup of the broth to the butter mixture, stirring constantly; then add the remaining hot broth to the bowl, stirring constantly.

(5) Stir in the salt, mustard, mace, ginger, garlic, and lemon slice.

(6) Return this mixture to the saucepan, and bring to a boil, still stirring; reduce the heat and simmer 5 to 10 minutes.

(7) Remove the garlic cloves and the lemon slice, and discard.

(8) Add the pepper and cayenne to the soup.

(9) Stir in the almonds, and simmer another two minutes.

(10) Add 1/2 cup of the cream to the soup.

NOTE: *If you desire a richer soup, add the remaining 1/2 cup of cream. Bring the mixture just to the boiling point and serve at once.*

INGREDIENTS

2 tablespoons of flour
1 tablespoon of butter
1 tablespoon of potato starch
4 1/2 cups of chicken broth
1/2 teaspoon of salt
1/4 teaspoon of dried mustard
pinch of mace
1/8 teaspoon of powdered ginger
2 garlic cloves
1 lemon slice
freshly ground pepper
pinch of cayenne pepper
1 cup of finely ground, blanched
    almonds
1/2 to 1 cup of heavy cream

SERVES 6-8

CREAM OF WILD RICE SOUP

(1) In a large pot, simmer the rice in the chicken broth until rice is soft.

(2) Strain off the rice, saving the broth. Set aside.

(3) In a skillet, sauté the celery, carrots, and onion in 2-3 tablespoons of butter.

(4) Cook, stirring, about 4-5 minutes, and drain off all the liquid.

(5) Set the vegetables aside.

(6) Make a roux in a pot by melting the 5 tablespoons of butter and whisking in the flour (over low to medium heat). Keep stirring, and do not let the mixture burn.

(7) Cook about 2 minutes.

(8) Add chicken broth and stir or whisk until smooth. If any lumps remain, just strain them out and discard.

(9) Add the vegetables and the rice and simmer 15 minutes, stirring occasionally.

(10) Add mushrooms and simmer another 5 minutes, stirring.

(11) Stir in the sherry and lemon juice, mixing well.

(12) In a small pot, heat the half-and-half, stirring, over medium heat, until it is reduced by half.

(13) Add half-and-half to the soup, along with salt and pepper to taste.

NOTE: *Serve with or without bacon on top.*

INGREDIENTS

1/2 cup of raw wild rice
5 cups of chicken broth
2 stalks of celery, chopped
3 carrots, peeled and sliced
1 onion, chopped
2-3 tablespoons of butter
5 tablespoons of butter for the
 roux
4 tablespoons of flour
1 cup of sliced, cleaned fresh
 mushrooms
1/2 cup of dry sherry
1 teaspoon of lemon juice
2 1/2 cups of half-and-half
salt to taste
freshly ground pepper

optional:

2-3 slices of cooked bacon to
 crumble on top

SERVES 4-6

CREAM OF MUSHROOM SOUP

(1) In a blender or food processor, combine the ricotta cheese with the milk, blending until smooth. Set aside.
(2) In a large kettle, over medium heat, heat the oil.
(3) Add the mushrooms and onions and cook, stirring frequently, for about 3-4 minutes.
(4) Remove the kettle from the heat and let the mushroom mixture cool thoroughly.
(5) Add the ricotta and milk mixture and stir for a minute or two.
(6) Return the entire mixture to the blender or food processor.
(7) Blend or process until smooth.
(8) Return the mixture to the kettle and add the chicken broth.
(9) Cook gently over low heat just until the soup is heated, stirring constantly.
(10) Do not allow the soup to boil. Add seasonings to taste and serve.

 INGREDIENTS

1 cup of ricotta cheese
1 cup of skim milk or 2% reduced fat milk
2 tablespoons of vegetable oil
3/4 pound of fresh mushrooms, wiped off and sliced
1 small onion, thinly sliced
2 cups of chicken broth
salt to taste
freshly ground pepper
pinch of nutmeg

NOTE: *This recipe has very little cholesterol.*

SERVES 4-6

CREAM OF SHALLOT SOUP

(1) In a large pot, melt the butter over low heat. Add the shallots and sauté for 10-15 minutes, stirring frequently.

(2) Add the flour and whisk it together quickly with the butter shallot mixture. Do not let the flour burn.

(3) Cook over low heat for 2 minutes.

(4) Slowly add the chicken broth, half-and-half, and cream.

(5) Stirring well, heat through, season with pepper and salt and serve.

 INGREDIENTS

6 tablespoons of butter
1 cup of minced shallots
4 tablespoons of flour
1 1/2 cups of chicken broth
2 1/2 cups of half-and-half
1 1/2 cups of whipping cream
freshly ground pepper
dash of salt

SERVES 8

CREAM OF
LEEK & GRUYÈRE SOUP

(1) In a large kettle or Dutch oven, combine 4 cups of the chicken broth, leeks, mushrooms, parsley, chives, tarragon, and pepper.

(2) Bring to a boil, reduce heat and simmer, covered, for about 12 minutes, or until leeks are tender.

(3) Place a third of the leek mixture in a blender or food processor (with the tube from the cover removed to let steam out), and blend until smooth.

(4) Repeat with the remaining mixture.

(5) Return all of the blended leek mixture to the kettle and stir in one of the remaining cups of chicken broth.

(6) Whisk together the flour and the remaining cup of chicken broth until smooth. Stir into the soup.

(7) Stir in the cheese and chopped parsley.

(8) Cook, stirring, for a few minutes, until cheese melts and soup begins to thicken slightly.

(9) Stir in cream, cook just until heated through. Serve immediately.

 INGREDIENTS

6 cups of chicken broth
4-6 leeks, washed and sliced
   (use white part only)
1/4 pound of fresh mushrooms,
   wiped and sliced
1/2 teaspoon of crushed parsley
1/4 teaspoon of dried chives
1/4 teaspoon of dried tarragon
freshly ground pepper
1/3 cup of all purpose flour
6 ounces of Gruyère cheese,
   shredded
2 tablespoons of fresh parsley,
   chopped
1 cup of whipping cream or half-
   and-half

NOTE: A great combination!

SERVES 6

ELAINE'S CREAM OF GARLIC SOUP

(1) Blend garlic in a food processor or blender until it is a coarse paste.
(2) Heat oil in a large heavy saucepan, over low heat.
(3) Add garlic paste and cook just until garlic begins to color.
(4) Stir frequently and cook for about 10-12 minutes.
(5) Add chicken broth and wine and bring to a boil.
(6) Reduce heat and simmer for 30 minutes, stirring occasionally.
(7) Add milk, cream and potato, and simmer, stirring occasionally, another 10 minutes.
(8) Purée soup, in small batches, in processor or blender, and strain into a saucepan.
(9) Return to a simmer and season with salt and pepper. Serve hot.

NOTE: *This soup can be made a day ahead.*

 INGREDIENTS

3/4 cup of peeled garlic cloves
3 tablespoons of olive oil
2 1/2 cups of chicken broth
1 cup of dry white wine
2 1/2 cups of whole milk
1 cup of whipping cream
1 russet potato, peeled and coarsely chopped
dash of salt
freshly ground pepper

SERVES 6

CREAM OF GREEN PEA SOUP

(1) In a saucepan, melt the butter and sauté the onion until soft and translucent.
(2) Stir in the curry powder, adding more to taste. Cook, stirring, for one minute.
(3) Add the uncooked peas, chicken broth, salt, and pepper.
(4) Cover and cook over medium heat for 5 minutes, until the peas are very soft.
(5) Pour the mixture into a blender or food processor, (no more than 2/3 full at a time) and purée until smooth.
(6) Add the cream and taste; adjust seasonings if necessary. Garnish if desired and serve.

 INGREDIENTS

2 tablespoons of butter
1 small onion, chopped
1-2 teaspoons (or more) of curry powder
21 ounces of green peas
4 cups of chicken broth
pinch of salt
freshly ground pepper
1/2 cup of heavy cream
garnish with whole green peas if desired

NOTE: *You can use frozen peas. Just make sure they are thawed and drained.*

SERVES 6-8

BLACK BEAN CHILI

(1) Heat the oil in a large pot.
(2) Sauté the onion and red pepper in the oil.
(3) Add the tomatoes, oregano, cumin, salt, and ground pepper. Cook for a few minutes over medium low heat and add the chopped green chilies, and garlic.
(4) Stir and cook for about 15 minutes and add the black beans.
(5) Continue cooking and stirring for another 20-30 minutes before adding the cilantro.
(6) Season with the lime juice before serving. Serve hot over brown rice.

NOTE: *If you cook this until it gets really thick, it makes a great dip.*

 INGREDIENTS

2 tablespoons of olive oil
1 medium onion, chopped
1 red pepper, stemmed, seeded, and diced
15 ounces of diced tomatoes
1 teaspoon of dried oregano
1 teaspoon of dried cumin
dash of salt
freshly ground pepper
4 ounces of chopped green chilies, mild
4 garlic cloves, minced
28 ounces of black beans
2 tablespoons of chopped cilantro
1 teaspoon of lime juice

SERVES 8

BLANQUETTE DE VEAU

(1) Place the veal in a large kettle, cover with cold water and bring to a boil.

(2) Boil the veal for 5 minutes, or until it turns white; drain, and rinse with fresh water.

(3) Return the meat to the kettle with fresh water and bring to a boil again.

(4) Add carrots, onions, leek, celery, the bouquet garni, salt and pepper to taste, and the garlic.

(5) Cover the kettle with waxed paper and a tight-fitting lid, and lower heat.

(6) Simmer veal, for 1 hour, or until tender. Do not overcook.

(7) When meat is done, remove it from the liquid and place it in a serving dish or casserole, reserving the cooking liquid. Reserve the liquid.

(8) Keep the meat warm while you complete the recipe.

(9) Gently heat the pearl onions in a small saucepan and add them to the veal.

(10) Strain the liquid, discarding the vegetables.

(11) Return the liquid to the kettle and cook over high heat until it is reduced to half its original quantity. You should end up with 2 cups of liquid–no more.

(12) Meanwhile, place the mushrooms in a small saucepan with the water, salt, lemon juice, and 1 tablespoon of butter.

(13) Bring to a boil and simmer gently for 4 minutes.

(14) Remove the saucepan from the heat and drain the mushrooms, reserving the cooking liquid.

(15) Add mushrooms to veal-onion mixture.

(16) In a medium saucepan, melt 2 tablespoons of butter over low heat, and add the flour, stirring constantly with a wire whisk.

(17) Add the veal cooking liquid and bring to a boil; then add the reserved mushroom cooking liquid to the sauce.

(18) Bring sauce to a boil again and cook for 15-20 minutes, or until the sauce has thickened and has a

creamy-smooth texture. (This reduction process is the secret of this marvelous sauce.)

(19) While the sauce is cooking, combine the remaining butter with the egg yolks and sour cream in a small bowl.

(20) Add a small portion of the sauce to this mixture, stirring rapidly; do not allow the egg yolks to curdle.

(21) Return the egg yolk mixture to the remaining sauce and stir vigorously for 5 minutes over medium heat.

(22) Pour the sauce over the veal mixture, and serve at once with boiled rice.

NOTE: *A rather complicated dish, but your patience will be rewarded with an exquisite entrée.*

 INGREDIENTS

2 1/2-3 pounds of boneless veal breast or shoulder, cut into 1-inch cubes
2 carrots, peeled and sliced
2 medium whole onions, pierced with 2 cloves
1 leek, sliced
1 stalk of celery with leaves
1 bouquet garni (1 bay leaf and 1 teaspoon of thyme leaves and 1 sprig of parsley all wrapped in cheese cloth)
pinch of salt and freshly ground pepper to taste
1 garlic clove, split
1 can (16 ounces) of pearl onions, drained
3/4 pound of fresh mushrooms, wiped and sliced
1/2 cup of water
1/2 teaspoon of salt
juice of 1/2 lemon
7 tablespoons of butter
3 tablespoons of flour
2 egg yolks
1/2 cup of sour cream

SERVES 6-8

BEEF BOURGUIGNON

Preheat the oven to 300° F.

(1) Drain the beef on paper towels, and dredge in the seasoned flour.

(2) In a large pot or Dutch oven, heat the oil, then brown the meat over high heat, adding more oil as needed.

(3) Remove meat as it browns. When all the beef has been browned, return it to the pot.

(4) Gently heat the brandy in a small pot, and ignite it.

(5) Pour flaming brandy over the meat, and when the flame dies out, remove beef from the pot and set aside.

(6) Heat a little more oil in the same pot or Dutch oven, and add the onions and mushrooms.

(7) Cook, stirring occasionally, for 5 minutes, or until onions begin to brown.

(8) Place beef, onions, and mushrooms in a 3 or 4 quart casserole.

(9) Add the wine, bouillon cubes, bay leaf, salt and pepper to taste.

(10) Place in the oven and cook, covered, for 2-3 hours, or until meat is tender.

(11) Remove bay leaf before serving.

NOTE: If the sauce gets too thick, add a little more wine. If the sauce is too thin, reduce by removing the cover for the last hour of cooking. Check the beef about every half hour. To prepare in advance: follow all steps, but about 3 hours before serving, remove from the refrigerator to let it warm up to room temperature. Gently reheat in a slow oven for 45 minutes to 1 hour.

 INGREDIENTS

3 pounds of stewing beef, cut into 1-inch cubes
1/2 cup of flour (approximately) seasoned with salt and pepper
4 tablespoons of olive oil
2 tablespoons of brandy
1 pound of whole, small white onions, peeled
3/4 pound of whole mushrooms, wiped
3 cups of red wine
2 beef bouillon cubes
   1 bay leaf
   pinch of salt
   dash of freshly ground pepper

SERVES 4-6

CHICKEN
IN CURRIED CREAM SAUCE

(1) Sprinkle chicken pieces with mixture of flour, curry powder, salt and pepper.

(2) Heat butter, add chicken, and brown on both sides. If necessary, add more butter.

(3) Add onion and cook gently for about 5 minutes.

(4) Pour in wine and cook on low until chicken is done, about 30 minutes or more.

(5) In a separate, small pan, sauté mushrooms in a little butter; then add them to the wine and chicken.

(6) Mix egg yolk and cream and gradually add some of the cooking liquid, stirring vigorously.

(7) Return mixture to the pot and heat gently, for a minute or two, shaking pan to coat the chicken.

 INGREDIENTS

3 pounds of chicken, cut into serving pieces
2 tablespoons of flour
1 tablespoon of curry powder
1 teaspoon of salt
dash of freshly ground pepper
3 tablespoons of butter
1 small onion, peeled and finely chopped
3/4 cup of white wine
1/2 pound of small mushrooms, wiped
1 egg yolk
1/4 cup of heavy cream

NOTE: *The curry powder gives this dish its unique flavor, but you do not need to worry about it being too hot like the Eastern curried dishes.*

SERVES 4-6

LAZY COOK'S BOUILLABAISSE

(1) In a large kettle or Dutch oven, heat the butter and add the onions and celery.

(2) Cook, stirring, over medium heat until the vegetables are soft but not brown.

(3) Add the tomatoes, fish, basil, Worcestershire sauce, and salt.

(4) Reduce the heat and cook, covered for 45 minutes, or until the fish is thoroughly cooked.

(5) During the last 5 minutes of cooking, drain the tuna, and add it to the kettle.

(6) Add the clams along with some of the liquid.

(7) Serve the stew in bowls accompanied by your favorite bread and salad. The stew can also be refrigerated for several days and gently reheated.

NOTE: Bouillabaisse is a specialty of the French port city of Marseilles.

 INGREDIENTS

1/4 cup of butter
1 large onion, finely chopped
1 cup of chopped celery
56 ounces of concentrated crushed tomatoes
2 pounds of boneless fish fillets (haddock, perch, cod or a mixture) cut into large chunks
1 teaspoon of basil
1 teaspoon of Worcestershire sauce
pinch of salt
6 1/2 ounces of tuna, packed in water
6 1/2 ounces of minced clams

NOTE: A real bouillabaisse is a work of art, but this quick version is quite simple to fix, and low in cholesterol, too.

SERVES 4-6

MUSHROOM BARLEY SOUP/STEW

(1) Heat the oil
(2) Add meat and bones, and brown.
(3) Add onions, mushrooms, and carrots; stir and cook over low heat for 10 minutes.
(4) Add barley, water, salt, and pepper. Bring to a boil, and skim off foam.
(5) Lower heat to a simmer, cover and cook for 2 1/2 hours or until the meat is tender.

 INGREDIENTS

2 tablespoons of vegetable oil
1 pound of short ribs, beef chuck ribs, or flanken
2 beef marrow bones
3 onions, peeled and chopped
1/2 pound of fresh mushrooms, wiped and sliced
6 carrots, chopped
1/2 to 1 cup of pearl barley, rinsed and drained
9 cups of water
1 tablespoon of salt
dash of freshly ground pepper

SERVES 4-6

JACK-O-'LANTERN STEW

Preheat the oven to 350° F.

(1) Wash and dry the pumpkin. Cut off the top, leaving a nice slice for the lid.

(2) Place the pumpkin in a large, shallow baking dish, and scoop out all the seeds (these may be baked separately for a nutritious snack).

(3) Combine the apples, raisins, pecans, water, sugar, lemon juice, lemon peel, cinnamon, and nutmeg in a medium saucepan, and bring to a boil, stirring for a minute or two.

(4) Pour the apple mixture into the pumpkin and cover it with the lid.

(5) Bake for 45-55 minutes at 350° F., or until the apples are tender.

(6) When serving, be sure to scoop out some of the pumpkin meat. This stew can be served hot or at room temperature.

 INGREDIENTS

1 small pumpkin
2-3 large tart apples, peeled and chopped
1 cup of yellow raisins
3/4 cup of chopped pecans
1/3 cup of water
1/3 cup of sugar
1 teaspoon of lemon juice
1 teaspoon of grated lemon peel (zest)
1/4 teaspoon of cinnamon
freshly grated nutmeg to taste

NOTE: A colorful side dish to serve with almost any autumn menu.

SERVES 6-8

CURRIED LAMB

(1) In a large kettle or Dutch oven, over medium heat, melt the butter and add the lamb.

(2) Cook the lamb, turning the pieces several times, until no pink shows on the outside of the meat.

(3) Add the onion, garlic, and apple wedges, stir, and continue cooking until most of the liquid has evaporated.

(4) Sprinkle the curry powder and flour over the meat mixture, and stir until the meat is well coated.

(5) Add the tomatoes, raisins, chicken broth, water, and salt and pepper. Bring to a boil.

(6) Lower the heat and simmer, covered, 1 to 1 1/2 hours, or until the meat is thoroughly tender.

(7) Skim off any fat, and stir in the cream and the optional coconut.

(8) Cook just until the cream is heated, but do not allow the sauce to boil.

(9) Taste and correct the seasonings. Serve with boiled white rice, and small bowls of any of the following condiments: chutney, chopped hard-boiled eggs, Spanish peanuts, mashed bananas, raisins, shredded coconut, and chopped onions.

NOTE: *The fun of serving this dish is setting out several condiments for your guests to place on top of the dish.*

 ## INGREDIENTS

6 tablespoons of unsalted butter

5 pound leg of lamb, boned and cut into 1-inch cubes

1 cup of finely chopped onion

1 garlic clove, finely chopped

1 apple, cored, peeled and cut into wedges

1/4 cup of curry powder (to taste)

2 tablespoons of flour

1 cup of peeled, chopped tomatoes

1/2 cup of raisins

1/2 cup of chicken broth

1 cup of water

dash of salt

dash of freshly ground pepper

1 cup of heavy cream

1 cup of shredded coconut (optional)

SERVES 6-8

COUSCOUS TAGINE

Preheat the oven to 350° F.

(1) Heat the oil in a large skillet and brown the meat (on the outside).
(2) Place the meat in a large kettle or Dutch oven.
(3) Add the apricots, raisins, and tomatoes. Cover and bake at 350° F. for 45 minutes, or until the meat is tender.
(4) Add the vegetables and enough chicken broth to cover the entire mixture. Bake another 20 to 30 minutes.
(5) Meanwhile, soak the couscous in cold water for 15 minutes.
(6) Drain and cook the couscous in a steamer until it is tender, about 10-15 minutes.
(7) Remove the couscous from the steamer and place it on a large platter.
(8) Lightly oil your hands with vegetable oil and roll the couscous between your palms so that each grain is separated and coated with oil.
(9) Return the couscous to the steamer and cook for another 10 minutes. Keep warm.

To Prepare the Harissa Sauce:

(1) Grind together (blender or mortar and pestle) the spices, garlic, and salt. (This mixture can be prepared at any time and kept in a tightly covered, glass jar in the refrigerator until needed.)
(2) A few minutes before serving, add the olive oil to the spice mixture, and place in a small saucepan.
(3) Cook, stirring constantly, for 5 minutes.
(4) Before serving the tagine, remove the cinnamon sticks and cloves and discard them.
(5) Garnish the tagine with currants and nuts.

NOTE: Serve the tagine, couscous, and sauce separately. Let your guests mix the 3 together as they choose.

INGREDIENTS

Tagine:

1/2 cup of olive oil
1 1/2 pounds of boneless meat, cut
   into large chunks
1/2 pound of dried apricots
1/2 pound of raisins
4 ripe tomatoes, peeled and cut into
   wedges
2 large onions, cut into wedges
4 carrots, peeled and thickly sliced
3 ribs of celery, cut into large pieces
16 ounces of garbanzo beans,
   drained
17 ounces of sweet potatoes, drained
6 artichoke hearts
chicken broth to cover
17 ounces of couscous
vegetable oil

Harissa Sauce:

3 cinnamon sticks
2 cloves, crushed
2 tablespoons of cayenne pepper
1 teaspoon of fennel seeds
1 teaspoon of caraway seeds
1 teaspoon of ground cumin
10 whole garlic cloves
1/2 teaspoon of salt
1 cup of olive oil

Garnish:

1/4 pound of dried currants
1/4 pound of chopped almonds
   or pine nuts

SERVES 6-8

JAMBALAYA

Preheat the oven to 325° F.

(1) Wash and dry the chicken pieces.
(2) In a large kettle or Dutch oven, heat the butter and oil over medium high heat.
(3) Brown the chicken pieces, a few at a time, until golden brown on all sides.
(4) Remove the pieces as they brown and place them in a large shallow baking dish.
(5) Bake chicken at 325° F. for 30 minutes.
(6) Meanwhile add more butter and oil to the kettle, if needed, and sauté the ham, green pepper, onion, and celery for about 5 minutes.
(7) Add the tomatoes, salt, bay leaf, garlic, Tobasco, red pepper, water, and optional corn to the kettle. Bring the mixture to a boil.

(8) Stir in the rice, cover, reduce heat and simmer over medium low heat for 20 minutes, or until all the liquid is absorbed.
(9) During the last 5 minutes of cooking time, add the shrimp and the baked chicken
(10) Let the jambalaya stand, covered, for 10 minutes, or until all the liquid is absorbed.
(11) Remove the bay leaf and discard. Taste for seasoning.

NOTE: Sensational and versatile. Add or subtract ingredients to suit your personal taste.

INGREDIENTS

3 frying chickens, cut into serving
   pieces
1/2 cup of butter
6 tablespoons of vegetable oil
3/4 pound of cooked ham, diced
1 green pepper, coarsely chopped
1 large onion, finely chopped
2 ribs of celery, cut in large
   chunks
4 tomatoes, peeled, seeded and
   chopped
1/2 teaspoon of salt
1 bay leaf
2 garlic cloves, finely chopped
dash of Tabasco sauce
1/2 teaspoon of dried, crushed red
   pepper
2 cups of water
10 ounces of frozen corn, thawed
   (optional)
1 1/2 cups of long grain, raw rice
1 pound of cooked shrimp,
   shelled and deveined

SERVES 8-10

LAMB RAGOUT

(1) Combine the flour, salt, and pepper in a paper or plastic bag.

(2) Add the cubed lamb and shake the bag vigorously to dredge the meat with the flour.

(3) In a heavy skillet, over medium high heat, heat the oil and sauté the lamb until brown on all sides; transfer meat to a large casserole as it browns.

Preheat the oven to 325° F.

(5) To the oil remaining in the skillet, add the garlic, onions, celery, carrot, and mushrooms.

(6) Sauté very lightly until the vegetables show just a trace of brown.

(7) Add the vegetables to the casserole, and in the same skillet, lightly brown the rice, adding a little more oil if needed.

(8) Add the rice to the casserole, along with the tomato, bay leaf, and oregano.

(9) Pour the stock (beef or chicken broth) and the wine into the skillet, and deglaze it, with a wire whisk, by scraping up any browned bits that have adhered to the bottom.

(10) Add this to the casserole, cover it tightly, and bake for 1 1/2 hours (at 325° F.) or until the meat is very tender and the rice has absorbed all of the liquid. If the rice has not absorbed all the liquid, remove the cover and let the casserole bake another 15 minutes.

(11) Discard the bay leaf and correct the seasonings before serving the dish garnished with the parsley.

NOTE: *A marvelous one-pot dish that needs only a tossed salad and perhaps a loaf of French bread to turn it into a very satisfying company meal.*

INGREDIENTS

1/4 cup of flour
1 teaspoon of salt
freshly ground pepper
2 1/2 pounds of shoulder of lamb,
  cut into 1 1/2-inch cubes
3 tablespoons of olive oil
1 garlic clove, crushed
2 medium onions, chopped
2 ribs of celery, chopped
1 carrot, peeled and chopped
1/2 cup of chopped fresh mushrooms
1 cup of long grain, raw white rice
2 tomatoes, peeled and coarsely
  chopped
1 bay leaf
1/2 teaspoon of oregano
1 cup of beef or chicken broth
1 cup of dry white wine
2 tablespoons of chopped parsley

SERVES 6

STOKES' BARBECUE

(1) Place the beef in a large kettle or Dutch oven along with the onions, celery, salt and pepper to taste, and enough water to cover the meat.

(2) Cover the kettle and cook the beef over medium low heat until the meat falls apart–about 3 hours.

(3) Drain off the water, and keep the meat warm.

(4) Prepare the barbecue sauce by combining all the ingredients in a blender or food processor, and blending until smooth.

(5) Transfer the mixture to a medium saucepan and cook over low heat, stirring occasionally until heated through.

(6) Add the sauce to the meat, mixing well.

NOTE: Serve with hard rolls or sourdough bread. Bill Stokes is a patent attorney, and one of the best male cooks I know!

 INGREDIENTS

3 to 4 pounds of boneless beef chuck roast, trimmed of fat
2 onions, finely chopped
1 rib of celery, finely chopped
dash of salt
freshly ground pepper

Barbecue Sauce

1/2 cup of butter, softened
2 tablespoons of cider vinegar
1 tablespoon of chili powder
1 teaspoon of ground cumin
2 cups of catsup
1 teaspoon of garlic powder
2 tablespoons of salad oil
1 teaspoon of dry mustard
dash of salt
pinch of cayenne pepper
1 tablespoon of lemon juice

SERVES 6-8

POULET MARENGO

(1) Wash and dry the chicken pieces.
(2) In a large Dutch oven or flameproof casserole, gently heat the oil over medium high heat.
(3) Add the garlic; cook. Discard when it browns.
(4) Add chicken pieces and sauté until brown on all sides.
(5) Add more oil if necessary, and when heated, add onions, tomatoes, mushrooms, tomato paste, wine, pepper, parsley, thyme, and salt.
(6) Bring to a boil, reduce heat, and simmer, covered for about 1 hour or until chicken is cooked and tender. If sauce is too thin, stir a little flour into a bowl with a little sauce and when smooth, stir mixture back into the pot.
(7) Simmer for 5 more minutes.

NOTE: *Great with noodles, French bread, and white wine. This dish was composed for Napoleon to celebrate one of his victories.*

 INGREDIENTS

3 pounds of chicken cut up into serving pieces
2 tablespoons of (or more) olive oil
1 garlic clove, peeled
2 onions, peeled and finely chopped
3 tomatoes, peeled and chopped
1/2-1 pound of fresh, small whole mushrooms, brushed off
6 ounces of tomato paste
2/3 cup of dry white wine
freshly ground pepper
pinch of fresh parsley
pinch of thyme
dash of salt

SERVES 6

YUCATAN CHICKEN

(1) Line a shallow baking pan with aluminum foil.

(2) Season the chicken with the chili and curry.

(3) Place the chicken in the prepared pan, and distribute the onions, tomatoes, celery, and green pepper over the chicken pieces.

(4) Pour the orange juice over everything and marinate in the refrigerator for several hours.

Preheat the oven to 300° F.

(5) Cover the pan tightly with foil, and bake chicken at 300° F. for 4 hours.

NOTE: *Slow cooking is most important to achieve the correct flavor and consistency. Serve with boiled white rice. This is an Americanized version of a popular Mexican dish.*

 INGREDIENTS

6-8 whole chicken breasts cut in half

2 tablespoons of chili powder (approximately)

2 tablespoons of curry powder (approximately)

1 large onion, finely chopped

3 medium tomatoes, peeled and chopped

3 ribs of celery, chopped

1 green pepper, chopped

4 cups of orange juice

SERVES 6-8

RATATOUILLE NICOISE

(1) In a large kettle, gently heat the olive oil over medium high heat.

(2) Add the garlic, onion, and green pepper, and sauté the mixture until the vegetables are tender but not brown.

(3) In a large bowl, toss the eggplant and zucchini with the flour and add this mixture to the kettle.

(4) Cover and cook over low heat for one hour, stirring occasionally.

(5) Meanwhile, peel the tomatoes and coarsely chop them.

(7) Place the tomatoes in a colander to drain off the excess liquid.

(8) After an hour, add the tomatoes to the kettle. Salt and pepper to taste.

(9) Cook uncovered for 15 minutes.

NOTE: The mixture should be very thick. The Ratatouille may be served hot, at room temperature, or chilled.

 INGREDIENTS

1/4 cup of olive oil
5-6 garlic cloves, crushed
1 medium onion, chopped
1 green pepper, seeded and cut into thin strips
1 small eggplant, unpeeled, cut into cubes
2 medium zucchini, cubed
1/4 cup of flour
3 large tomatoes
dash of salt
freshly ground pepper

NOTE: A great vegetarian dish.

SERVES 6-8

NEW ENGLAND
CLAM CHOWDER

(1) All clams should be tightly shut when you buy them. Scrub clams and place in a 4-quart kettle or Dutch oven.

(2) Pour in enough wine to measure about 1/2 inch deep.

(3) Cover and cook clams on medium heat, shaking the pot occasionally, for about 10-20 minutes, or until clams open.

(4) Discard any clams that have not opened.

(5) Strain the liquid through a fine sieve lined with a paper towel.

(6) Save the liquid. If it measures less than 4 cups, add enough water to make 4 cups of liquid.

(7) Remove clams from the shells, and cut in half. Mince any hard pieces.

(8) Rinse out the kettle and cook the bacon. Remove the bacon when it is done, and leave about 2 tablespoons of the fat.

(9) Sauté the onion in the bacon fat for about 5 minutes.

(10) Stir in the potatoes, pepper, salt, thyme, and Tabasco.

(11) Add the 4 cups of clam liquid.

(12) Cook over medium to low heat until potatoes are tender, about 10-15 minutes.

(13) Add the cream, clams, bacon and butter.

(14) Stir and cook, adjusting the seasoning if necessary.

(15) Add cognac, stir and serve.

NOTE: If canned clams have to be
used, purchase 2 or 3, 7 1/2 or
8-ounce cans, drain the liquid in
a large measuring cup, adding
enough wine or water to make 2
cups of liquid. Then use a cup of
bottled clam juice and a cup of
water to makeup the other 2 cups
of liquid.

INGREDIENTS

2 dozen medium-sized chowder
  clams
dry white wine, or water
4 slices of bacon, diced
1 onion, finely chopped
4 medium potatoes, cut into
  1/2-inch diced pieces
freshly ground pepper
dash of salt
pinch of thyme
dash of Tabasco
4 cups of liquid from the clams
2 cups of heavy cream, or half-
  and-half
2 tablespoons of butter

1-2 tablespoons of Cognac
  (optional)

SERVES 4-6

LEEK & POTATO CHOWDER

(1) Scrub dirt and sand from the clams.

(2) In a large pot, bring 2 cups of water to a boil. Add clams. (with seasoning, if desired).

(3) When clams open, remove pot from heat, remove clam meat from the shells (discard shells), and dice the meat. Set the meat aside to cool. Save the clam liquid.

(4) Chop leeks and place them in the clam liquid along with the potatoes, garlic, and sherry.

(5) Bring to a boil and reduce heat to simmer. Simmer covered for about 10 minutes or until potatoes are soft.

(6) Remove from heat, strain off the broth, cool.

(7) Purée the vegetables and a little broth in a blender or a food processor.

(8) Return to the pot and add cream, butter, salt and pepper to taste, and clams.

(9) Heat for another minute or two until warm.

 INGREDIENTS

8 large chowder clams
2 cups of water
1/2 teaspoon of Bay seasoning (optional)
6 large leeks, without green
2 medium potatoes, peeled and cubed
2 garlic cloves, finely chopped
1/4 cup of sweet yellow sherry
1/4 cup of whipping cream
2 tablespoons of butter
dash of salt
freshly ground pepper

NOTE: Great garnished with avocado slices. This can be reheated, gently, but does not freeze well because of the potatoes.

SERVES 6-8

ASPARAGUS LEEK CHOWDER

(1) In a large saucepan, sauté mushrooms, leeks, and asparagus in butter until tender, about 8-10 minutes.

(2) Stir in flour, salt, and pepper.

(3) Add broth and cream, stirring until mixture is thick and bubbly.

(4) Stir in the corn and crushed saffron. Do not boil, but continue to heat through on low.

(5) Season to taste with additional salt and pepper.

 INGREDIENTS

8 ounces of fresh mushrooms, wiped clean and sliced
3 large leeks, sliced
10 ounces of cut asparagus
6 tablespoons of butter
3 tablespoons of flour
dash of salt
freshly ground pepper
2 cups of chicken broth
2 cups of light cream
12 ounces of white, whole kernel corn
dash of crushed saffron

SERVES 6-8

MANHATTAN CLAM CHOWDER

(1) In a large kettle, sauté the bacon until it is almost done.
(2) Add the onions and cook until tender for about 5 minutes.
(3) Stir in the carrots, celery, potatoes, tomatoes, and fish broth or water.
(4) Bring to a boil; cover, reduce heat and simmer 15 minutes.
(5) Add clams and their juice, and clam juice.
(6) Add salt, pepper, and parsley if desired.
(7) Turn off the heat and let the soup stand for 30-45 minutes. Serve hot.

NOTE: *The "other way" to make clam chowder.*

 INGREDIENTS

4 slices of bacon, diced
2 onions, chopped
4-5 carrots, diced
3 ribs of celery, chopped
3-4 medium potatoes, chopped
1 3/4 pounds of tomatoes
2 cups of fish broth or water
1 pint of shucked clams, minced with juice
1 pint of bottle clam juice or water
dash of salt
freshly ground pepper
1 tablespoon of chopped parsley

SERVES 8

CORN CHOWDER

(1) In a large saucepan, sauté bacon until done.

(2) Add onion, and sauté 5 minutes.

(3) Stir in the potatoes, and 1 cup water.

(3) Cover and bring to a boil.

(4) Reduce heat and simmer for 10 minutes, or until potatoes are tender.

(5) Remove cover, and remove pan from heat. Set aside.

(6) In another saucepan, combine the corn, cream, sugar, and butter.

(7) Simmer, covered over low heat for 10 minutes.

(8) Add the potato mixture, salt, pepper, and 2 cups of milk.

(9) Cook, stirring occasionally over low heat until soup is heated but do not boil. Serve hot.

NOTE: *Gently reheat before serving, but do not boil.*

 INGREDIENTS

4 slices of bacon, finely chopped
1 medium onion, sliced thin
4 medium potatoes, peeled, and cubed
1 cup of water
4 cups of fresh corn kernels
1 cup of heavy cream or half-and-half
1 teaspoon of sugar
1/4 cup of butter
dash of salt
freshly ground pepper
2 cups of milk

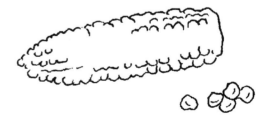

SERVES 8-10

BASIC BEEF STOCK

Preheat the oven to 425° F.

(1) Sprinkle beef bones with sugar and bake in a baking pan until browned.

(2) Add bones to a large kettle or Dutch oven along with the carrots, onions, celery, parsley, bay leaves, cloves, and enough water to cover all the solid ingredients.

(3) Bring the liquid to a boil. Skim off any residue.

(4) Lower the heat and simmer for 3 hours. Strain.

(5) Chill and remove solid fat.

NOTE: Many culinary institutions teach that no salt or pepper should be added to stock due to its high concentration; and as you don't know what soups the stock will be used for, add salt and pepper when you create the recipe.

 INGREDIENTS

3 pounds of beef bones, cracked
2 tablespoons of sugar
4 carrots, chopped coarsely
2 whole onions, cut into quarters
2 ribs of celery
1/3 cup of chopped parsley
1-2 bay leaves
2 whole cloves
3 quarts of cold water (approximately)

NOTE: Stock may be frozen for several months.

MAKES ABOUT 3 QUARTS

FISH STOCK

(1) Combine the fish, carrots, celery, onion, bay leaf, parsley, lemon juice, and dry vermouth or wine in a large kettle and allow liquid to simmer, uncovered, until reduced by half.
(2) Add water and bring to a boil.
(3) Reduce heat and simmer for another 20 minutes.
(4) Strain.

NOTE: *The easiest stock to prepare, and the most economical.*

 INGREDIENTS

2 pounds of fish heads, bones, and trimmings of flounder, sole, haddock, etc.
1-2 carrots, scraped and sliced
2 ribs of celery with leaves, chopped
1 large onion, peeled and chopped
1 bay leaf
1 sprig of fresh parsley
1 tablespoon of lemon juice
1 cup of dry vermouth or 1 1/2 cups of dry white wine
2 quarts of cold water

MAKES 8 CUPS OF STOCK

BASIC CHICKEN STOCK

(1) Place all ingredients in a large kettle or Dutch oven.
(2) Cover ingredients with cold water.
(3) Bring liquid to a boil. Skim off any residue that rises to the surface.
(4) Reduce heat and simmer, uncovered, for about 2 hours.
(5) Strain the solids from the stock and discard them.
(6) Remove fat from the surface (after refrigeration).

NOTE: Stock may be frozen for up to several months.

 INGREDIENTS

3 pounds of chicken necks, backs, wings, and giblets (no liver)
1 whole onion, peeled and stuck with 2 whole cloves
2 garlic cloves, crushed slightly (optional)
2 celery ribs with leaves, coarsely chopped
2 carrots, chopped coarsely
1 sprig of fresh parsley
cold water to cover

MAKES 6 CUPS OF STOCK

VEGETABLE BROTH MIX

(1) Combine all the ingredients and
    mix well.
(2) Store in a jar with a tight fitting
    lid. Stir well before each use.

*NOTE: Use 1 rounded teaspoonful to
each cup of water*

*NOTE: When a soup recipe calls for
vegetable broth mix, you can either
buy the ready made mix or make
your own. This is a basic mix, but
you can alter it by adding your
own favorite spices.*

 INGREDIENTS

1 tablespoon of onion powder
1 tablespoon of dried parsley
    flakes
1 1/2 teaspoons of garlic powder
1 1/2 teaspoons of celery
dash of salt
1/2 teaspoon of ground sage
1/2 teaspoon of dried marjoram
1/2 teaspoon of dried thyme
1/2 teaspoon of dried basil
1/2 teaspoon of dried oregano
1/4 teaspoon of pepper
1/4 teaspoon of turmeric
1/4 teaspoon of dill weed

MAKES 12 SERVINGS

INDEX

Traditional Country Life Recipe Books from
BRICK TOWER PRESS

Forthcoming titles:

Clambake
Cranberry Companion
Fresh Bread Companion
Fresh Vegetable Companion
Pies

Other titles in this series:

American Chef's Companion
Chocolate Companion
Fresh Herb Companion
Thanksgiving Cookery
Victorian Christmas Cookery
Apple Companion
Pumpkin Companion

MAIL ORDER AND GENERAL INFORMATION

Many of our titles are carried by your local book store or gift and museum shop. If they do not already carry our line please ask them to write us for information.

If you are unable to purchase our titles from your local shop, call or write to us.
Our titles are available through mail order. Just send us a check or money order for $9.95 per title with $1.50 postage (shipping is free with 3 or more assorted copies) to the address below or call us Monday through Friday, 9 AM to 5PM, EST. We accept Visa and Mastercard.

Send all mail order, book club, and special sales requests to the address below or call us for a free catalog. We can mail our catalog to you or e-mail a paper-free copy. In any case we would like to hear from you.

Brick Tower Press
1230 Park Avenue, 10th Floor
New York, NY 10128

Brick Tower Press, UK distribution
145 Springdale Road, Corfe Mullen
Wimborne, Dorset BH21 3QQ

Telephone & Facsimile
1-212-427-7139
1-800-68-BRICK

Telephone & Facsimile
(01202) 692045

E-mail
bricktower@aol.com